3 0007 00343 978 2

WITHDRAWN
FROM STOCK

SCIENCE
Quest

FORCES

CONTENTS

FORCES AND WORK

What is a force?

Forces can make objects move faster.

Forces can change the direction of movement.

Gravity is a force. It pulls objects towards the centre of the Earth.

A single pulley can be used to lift an object to a high place.

Friction is a force. It can make objects difficult to move.

Pulleys make heavy objects easier to lift.

Forces can slow objects down or stop them.

Forces can make objects move.

Levers are used to make objects easier to lift.

Work can be done to overcome gravity. We do this when we lift objects.

Forces can change the shape of materials.

SUMMARY

A force is either a push or a pull.

A force can make something move or stop, go faster or slower, or change direction.

A force can change the shape of an object.

When we lift something, we work against gravity.

Pulleys and levers are simple machines which help us to do work.

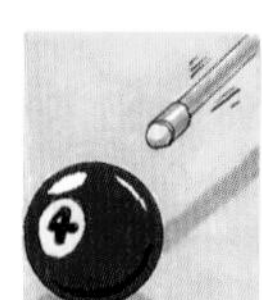

MOVING OBJECTS

Forces make objects move – and stop them moving

When a force is applied to a stationary object it tries to make the object move. If the object is already moving, the force will change its speed or direction.

The pool cue applies a force to the ball which causes it to roll across the table.

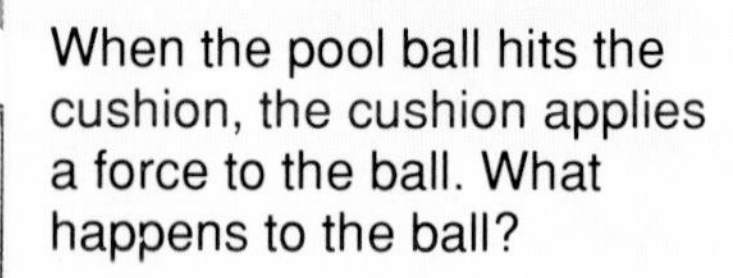

When the pool ball hits the cushion, the cushion applies a force to the ball. What happens to the ball?

When the dart hits the dart board, the dart board applies a force to the dart. What happens to the dart?

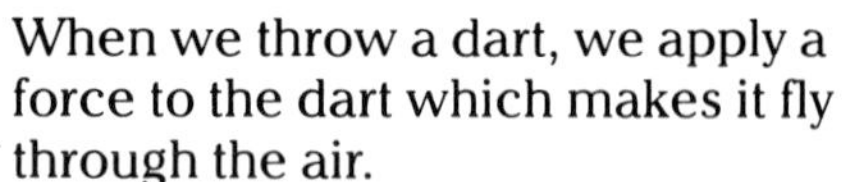

When we throw a dart, we apply a force to the dart which makes it fly through the air.

Just as we must apply a force to make things move, we must also apply a force to stop things moving. When we use brakes on a bicycle, we apply a force to stop the wheels turning. When the brakes are used, they become hot. Materials used to make brakes must be able to stand high temperatures.

Forces often act in pairs. If we try to push a heavy box across the floor, there is another force which seems to act against us. This force is called **friction** and is caused by the weight of the box holding it against the floor.

The amount of force caused by friction depends on how hard we push the box. If the box doesn't move, the frictional force must be the same as the force we are applying to push the box.

As we push harder, the friction increases. At a certain point, the friction is overcome and the box starts to move.

Investigation

Using a plastic box, some weights and some different surfaces, how could you investigate the friction between the box and the surfaces?

SUMMARY

Forces tend to make things move in the direction of the force.

Forces must be applied to stop things moving.

Friction is a force which tends to stop things moving.

LEVERS

How to move a heavy object

When we lift an object, we are applying a force. The force we apply is called the **effort**. The weight of the object is called the **load**.

Isaac Newton (1642–1727) is said to have worked out his laws of motion and gravity after considering why apples fall from trees.

Forces are measured in **newtons (N)**. A newton is the force which you would feel pressing down on your hand if you held an object such as an apple which weighed 100 g.

The weight of the box of apples in the picture opposite is a downwards force. This is the load which the boy is trying to move. The force applied by the boy is the effort.

What would happen to the effort needed to lift the apples if the pivot were moved closer to the apples?

The apples are too heavy for the children to move, but a piece of wood used as a lever and a log as a **pivot** can make the apples easy to lift.

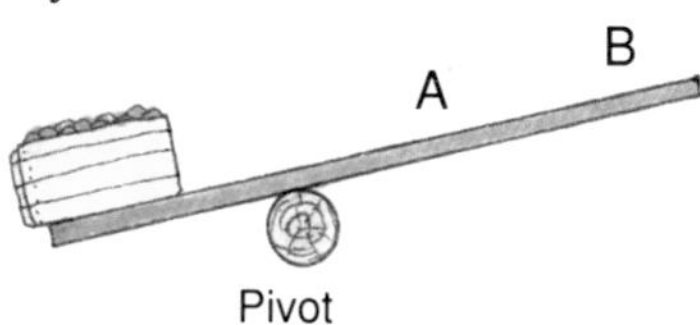

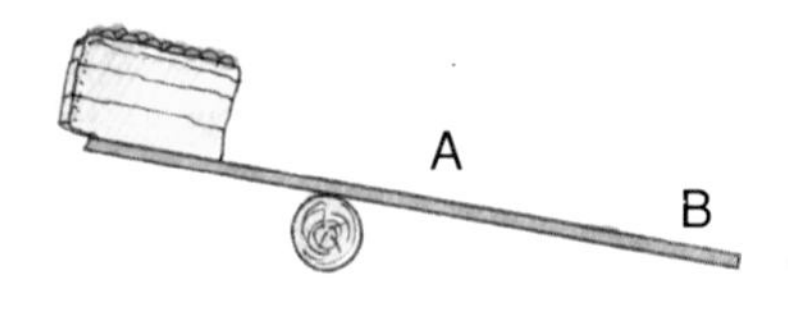

When we use a lever, we apply a force at a certain distance from the pivot. The effectiveness of the lever depends on both the force and the distance from the pivot at which the force is applied.

If the girl were to push down at point A would it be easier or harder to lift the apples than pushing down at point B?

Does A or B move farthest when the girl pushes down on the wood?

The **moment** of a force is found by multiplying the force by its distance from the pivot. The larger the moment, the more effective the lever will be in lifting the load.

Moment = Force × Distance

The standard unit for moment is newtons multiplied by metres. This unit is called a **joule (J).**

If a force of 20 N is applied at a distance of 3 m from the pivot, the moment is calculated as :

Moment = 20 × 3 = 60 Nm = 60 J

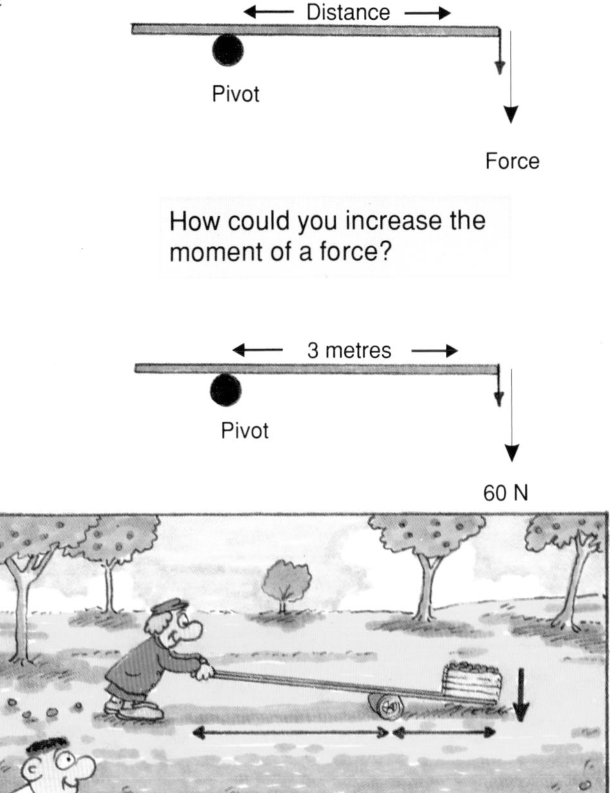

How could you increase the moment of a force?

To find out if a lever will lift a load, we have to work out the moments on both sides of the pivot. The moment due to the load is the weight exerted by the load multiplied by its distance from the pivot.

The moment due to the girl's effort is the force applied multiplied by its distance from the pivot. The lever will lift the load if the moment due to the person is greater than the moment due to the load.

Will the girl be able to use the lever to lift the load if she applies a force of 60 N at a distance of 2 m from the pivot?

What would happen if the moments were equal?

How many levers can you see in this picture?

SUMMARY

The force applied to lift a load is called the effort.

The moment of a force is the force multiplied by the distance from the force to the pivot.

Moments are measured in joules.

The greater the moment, the more effect the force will have on the lever.

When a lever is balanced, the moments are equal and act in opposite directions (the lever doesn't move).

FORCES AND TURNING

How forces can make objects rotate

When this bus driver wishes to turn left or right, she pulls the steering wheel with one hand and pushes it with the other.

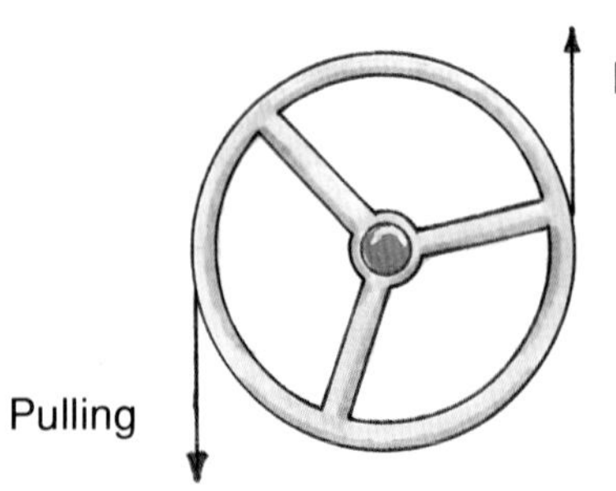

Could the driver turn the steering wheel with one hand?

Would it be harder to do this?

Would the wheel turn if both hands were pushing?

Why do you think a wider steering wheel is easier to turn?

Each force acting on the wheel produces a moment which tends to turn the wheel. As with levers, the moment is the force multiplied by the distance from the pivot. In this case the pivot is the centre of the steering wheel.

Buses have a wide steering wheel to increase the moments of the forces and make the steering wheel easier to turn.

Using two hands to turn the steering wheel produces a greater **turning effect** than one hand as there are two forces to turn the wheel, one pushing and one pulling.

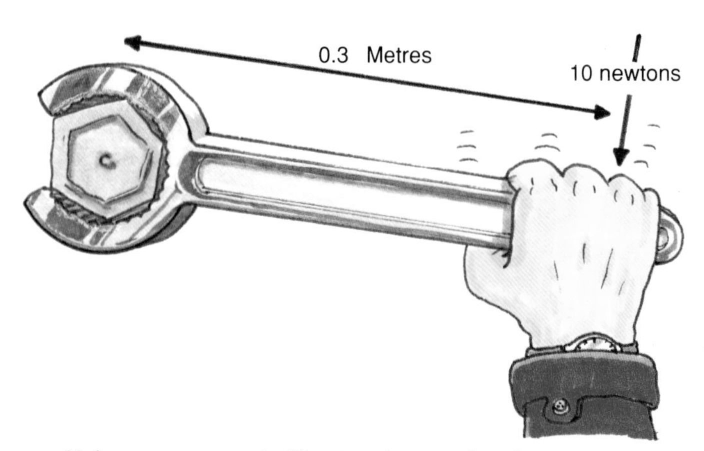

Using a spanner is like turning a wheel because the spanner moves in a circle around a nut. The nut is the pivot.

What is the value of the moment of the force turning the spanner?

Would a longer spanner have a larger or smaller moment?

The wheels of a vehicle rotate because of forces produced by the engine. The more force used, the faster the wheels spin and the faster the vehicle goes.

Forces are also applied to the wheels in order to stop the vehicle. The faster the vehicle is travelling, the more force is required to stop it.

When brakes are used on a vehicle, brake pads come into contact with the wheels which create enormous frictional forces. The moments of these forces are opposite to the direction the wheels are turning and so tend to stop the vehicle.

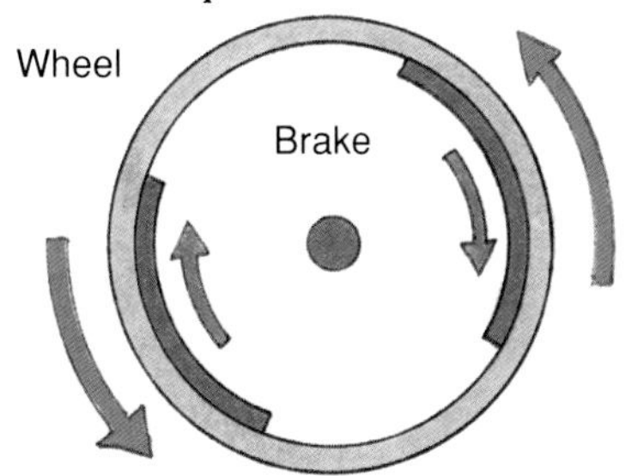

Brake drum of a car. The brake pads push outwards against the inside of the wheel.

The driver in the picture below has tried to stop too suddenly and his wheels have skidded along the road. The tyres must have a good grip on the road for the brakes to be effective.

Where are the forces applied to stop the car?

Why are the brakes of a motorcycle smaller than those of a car?

The weight of a vehicle also affects how difficult it is to stop. The heavier the vehicle, the more force is required to stop it.

SUMMARY

Turning forces often act in pairs.

The amount of effort needed to rotate an object depends on the perpendicular distance between the turning forces and the pivot.

The force needed to stop a vehicle depends on the speed and weight of the vehicle.

The forces which stop a vehicle are applied at the brakes and also between the tyres and the road.

PULLEYS

Lifting made easy

A **pulley** can be used to change the direction of a force. To lift the box upwards, the boy pulls downwards on the rope.

The force applied by the boy to the rope is the **effort**. If the effort is greater than the load, the box will lift.

What is the load in this picture?

In which direction is the effort being applied?

If the load is too heavy to lift by a single pulley, a different system of connected pulleys can be used. In this system, there are two pulleys. The top pulley is called the **block** and the bottom one is called the **tackle.**

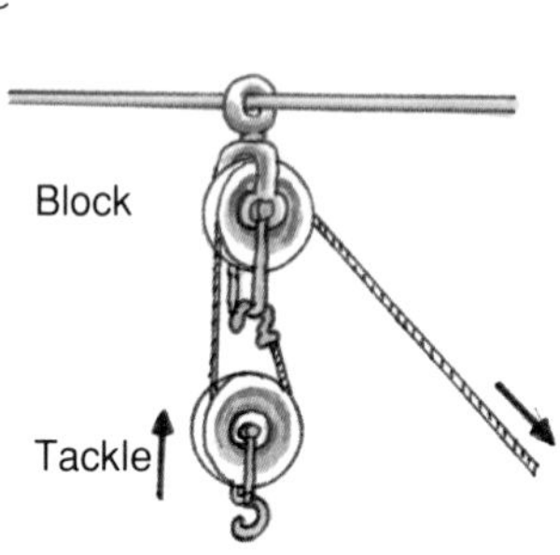

In this system the effort required to lift the load is about half of the weight of the box.

If the boy pulls the rope 1 m, how far does the weight move?

Cut away diagram of a tackle

An advantage of using a pulley is that heavy loads can be lifted more easily. There is a disadvantage, however, that the rope must be longer and must be pulled much further.

Using more pulleys can greatly increase the load which can be lifted by the effort.

This pulley system has three pulleys in the block and three in the tackle. It can be used to lift very heavy weights.

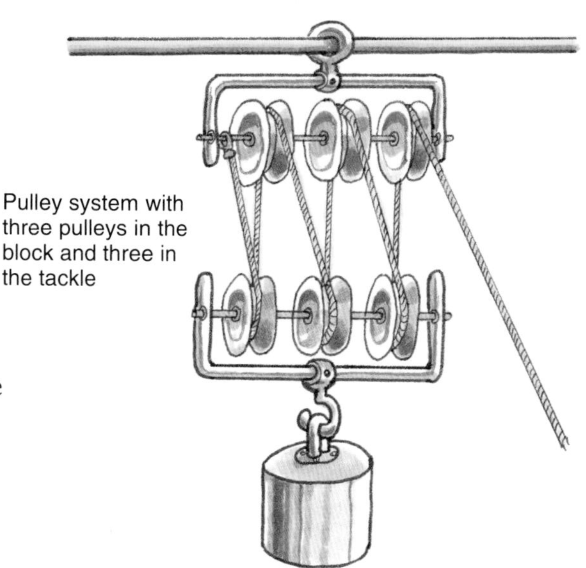

Pulley system with three pulleys in the block and three in the tackle

If this pulley system were used the effort would be about one-sixth of the weight. In fact the effort is slightly greater than one-sixth because we also need to lift the pulleys. The load includes the weight of the pulleys in the tackle.

Where might a pulley system like this be used?

How far would we have to pull the rope to lift the weight 1 m off the ground?

Can you think of any problems we would have lifting the load 20 m from the ground?

SUMMARY

Pulleys are often used when we have to lift a load to a high place.

A system of pulleys can reduce the effort needed to lift the load.

A pulley system usually has a block which is fixed and a tackle which moves with the load.

The weight of the tackle is part of the load.

Pulley systems do not make less work but allow us to use smaller forces to lift heavy things.

The disadvantage of pulley systems is that the rope must be pulled much further.

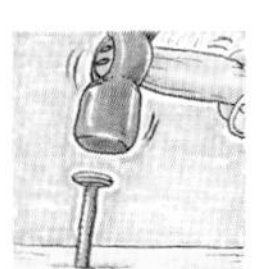

FORCES AND SHAPE

How forces can change the shape of an object

When gravity acts on an object, it tries to pull the object towards the centre of the Earth. When someone is standing on the floor, he or she is exerting a downward force on the floor. The force is caused by gravity and is called **weight.** Here the floor is supporting the person (and the apple) and is exerting an equal and opposite force upwards.

If the weight of the person was more than the upward force of the floor, what would happen?

When a force is applied to an object, it often causes the object to move. But sometimes the force causes the object to change shape.

Floors are designed to be strong enough to support people's weight without breaking or changing shape. Other materials may not be able to push back enough. For instance, if someone treads on an apple it will be crushed out of shape.

What does this tell you about the forces holding the apple in shape?

What word describes the ability of an object to keep its shape when a force acts on it?

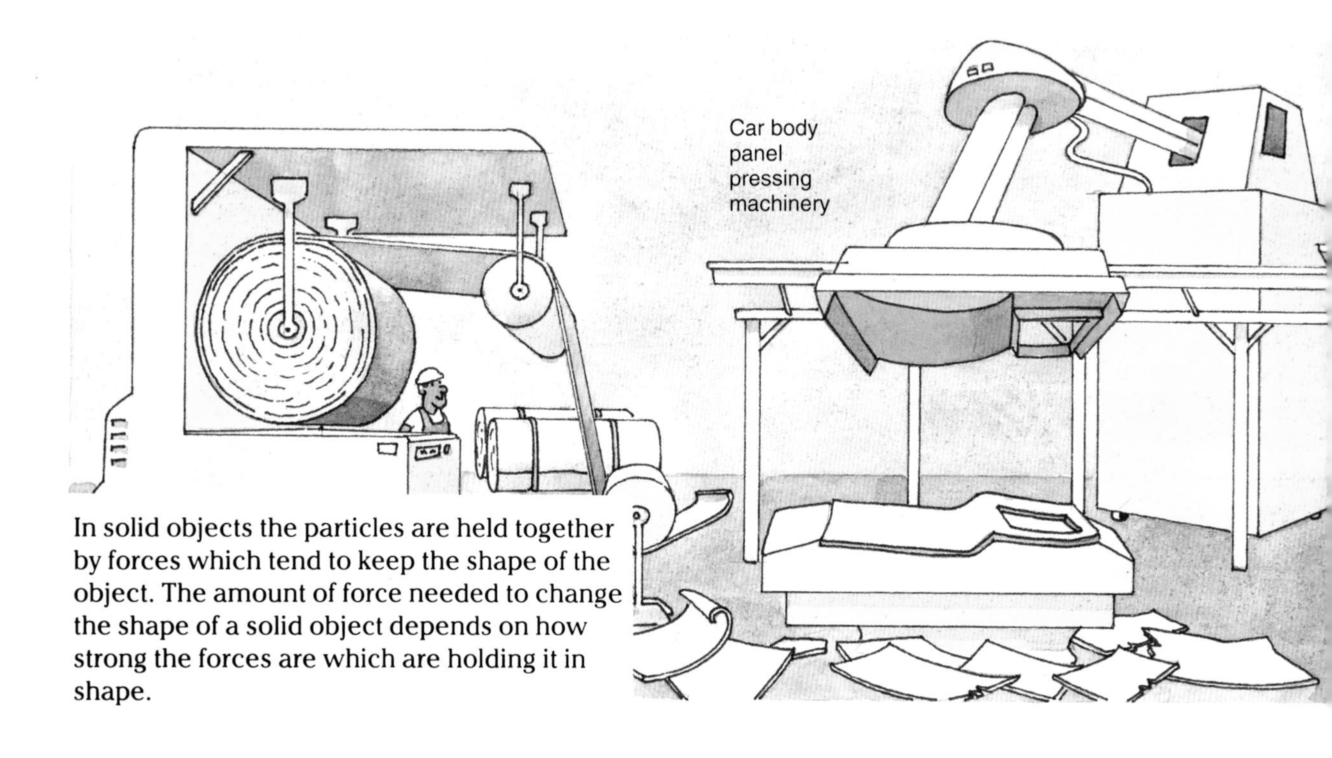

In solid objects the particles are held together by forces which tend to keep the shape of the object. The amount of force needed to change the shape of a solid object depends on how strong the forces are which are holding it in shape.

Some materials and objects have the ability to return to their original shape after being changed or **deformed** by a force.

This slow-motion sequence shows what happens when a football is kicked.

Just before contact, the ball is a sphere.

The ball deforms at the point of contact as it absorbs the force from the boot.

The ball returns to its original shape soon after it has been kicked.

The distance a football will fly depends on the force of the kick, the springiness of the ball and the length of time the force is in contact with the ball.

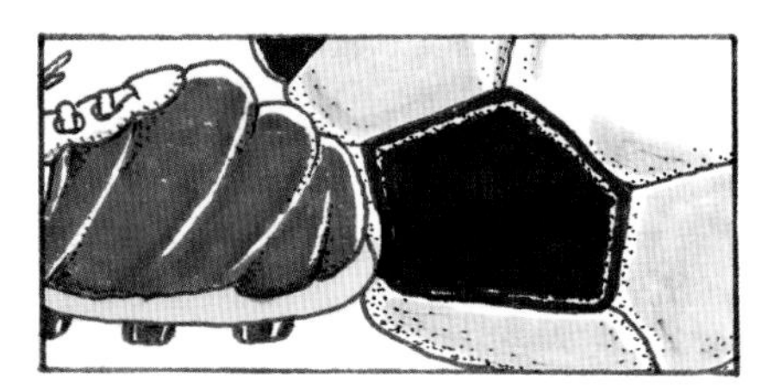

This ability of some objects to return to their original shape is called springiness, or **elasticity.**

The air inside a football helps to make the football springy. The shape of the metal in a coil spring helps to make it springy.

If a spring is attached to an object, the object can absorb a force more slowly.

Why do you think a burst ball can't be kicked as far as if it were fully inflated?

How many everyday uses for elasticity can you think of?

Is there any elasticity in a football boot?

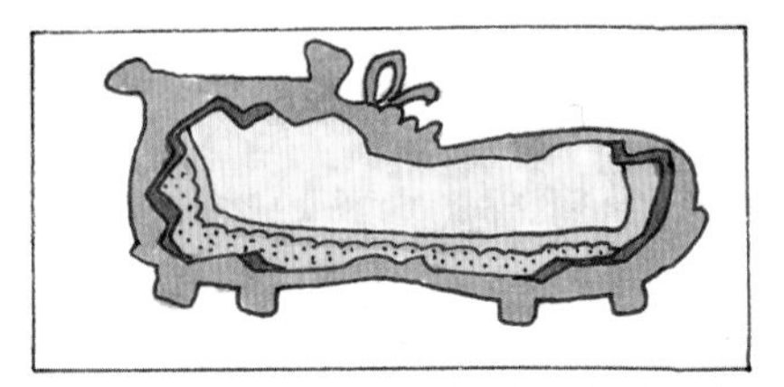

What would eventually happen to a car with no springs if it were driven fast on a bumpy surface?
Explain your answer.

SUMMARY

Some materials change shape when a force is applied to them.

When a force is applied to an elastic object, the application of the force tends to be spread over a long time compared to a non-elastic object.

Elasticity allows objects such as cars to be protected from forces which might otherwise cause damage.

BENDING THINGS

How forces affect materials

You can see what happens when you bend things. Draw lines on a piece of foam plastic, and then bend it.

What has happened to the spacing of the lines on the inside of the bend?

Where the lines are closer it is said to be under **compression**.

What other words might you use for compression?

Foam plastic bends easily. It's described as **flexible**. Materials which do not bend easily are described as **rigid** or **stiff**.

Can you think of some examples of rigid materials? Look around the room and make a list.

What happens if you try to bend these rigid materials?

The forces acting on this bridge are similar to the forces acting on your piece of foam plastic.

Reinforced concrete is strong under both tension and compression. The concrete is strong under compression and the steel reinforcing rods inside it are strong under tension. Without reinforced concrete many large modern structures would be impossible.

Look again at the piece of foam plastic. Where the plastic is stretched it is said to be under **tension**.

What has happened to the spacing on the outside of the bend?

Is concrete rigid or flexible?

This piece of concrete is being bent under enormous force.

Is the concrete under too much tension, or too much compression?

This damp piece of wood is also being bent.

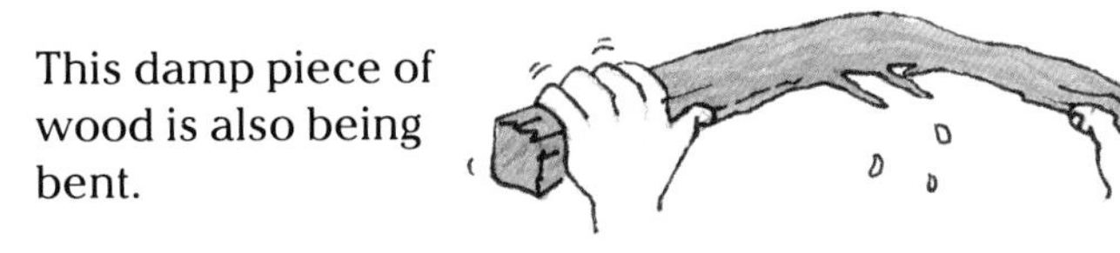

How would you describe what has happened to the piece of wood?

Investigation

How might a force such as your weight affect these three materials?

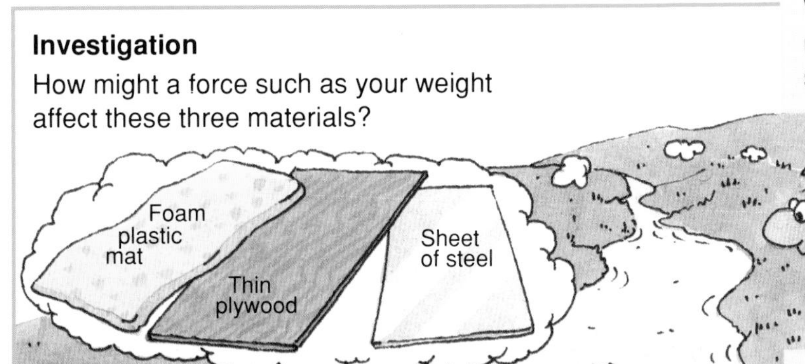

Which might be the best material to use for a simple bridge across this stream?

If you had to test your prediction, how would you do it?

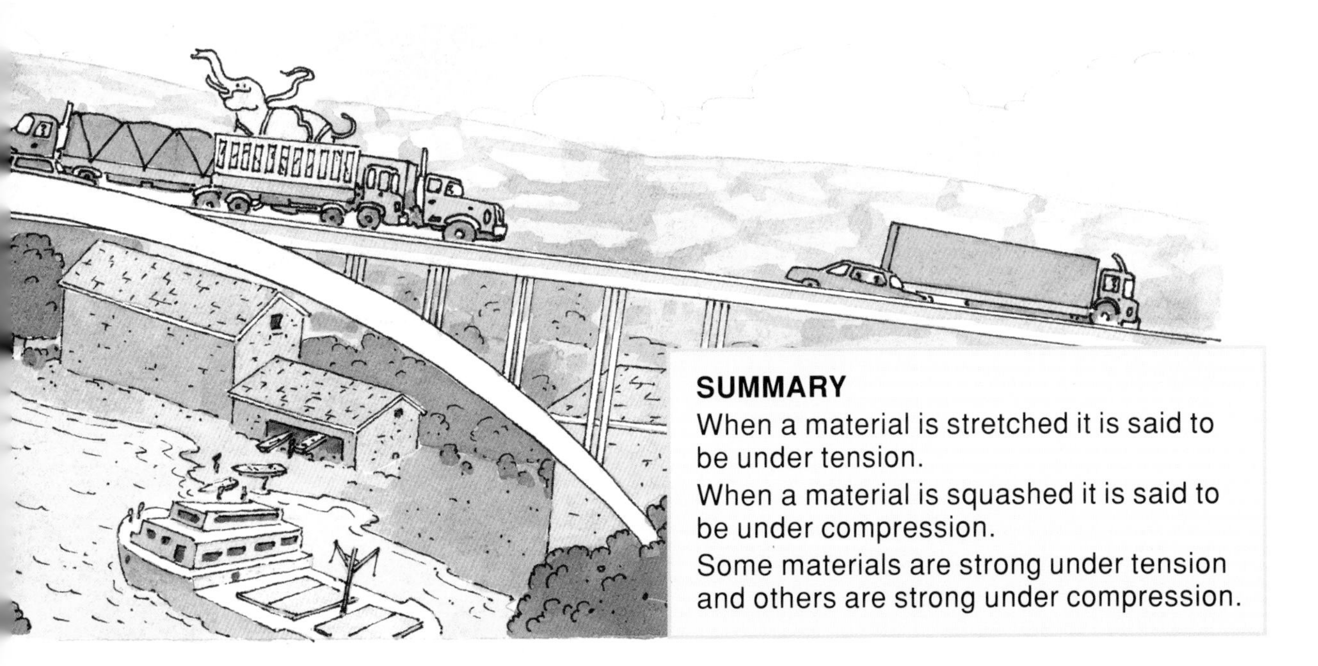

SUMMARY

When a material is stretched it is said to be under tension.

When a material is squashed it is said to be under compression.

Some materials are strong under tension and others are strong under compression.

BUILDING BRIDGES

How bridges are designed to use or withstand forces

Engineers have to take account of the forces of compression and tension when designing bridges. They have to choose materials which are suitable. A simple, short bridge can be made of one length of material, such as a wooden plank.

The Stone Age 'Post Bridge' in Devon is made up of a single stone slab supported by smaller stones.

Stone slabs are very hard but will not bend much without breaking. The strength under compression of stone can be used to build **arches**. Wedge-shaped blocks are slotted together to form a hump-backed bridge. The part of the bridge on which people or vehicles travel is called the **deck**. When something heavy travels across the deck of a stone bridge, the stones are forced together more tightly.

The particles in stone are similar to concrete particles.

Do you think a long slab of stone is strong under compression?

This ancient Roman single-arch bridge is near Colne in Lancashire.

What is supporting the weight of the monks?

What is supporting the bridge?

Simple arches are good for spanning short distances. But a huge amount of material has to be used to span long distances and to make the deck flat.

The Roman bridge at Nimes, France, is made up of many arches joined together.

Sydney Harbour Bridge has the deck slung beneath the steel arch on steel hanging rods.

When cheap steel became available in the nineteenth century, arch bridges could be made with less material. Steel is strong under both tension and compression, and can be used in long, connected sections.

What part of Sydney Bridge is under compression?

What parts are under tension?

About 80 per cent of the strength of the materials of a bridge is used to support the bridge itself. An arch bridge spanning say, 1 km would have to contain a huge amount of materials. This would increase the cost of the bridge.

Suspension bridges are used to span very large distances. The Humber Suspension Bridge, England has the world's longest single span at 1410 m. Huge steel cables attached to the banks and slung over concrete towers support the deck.

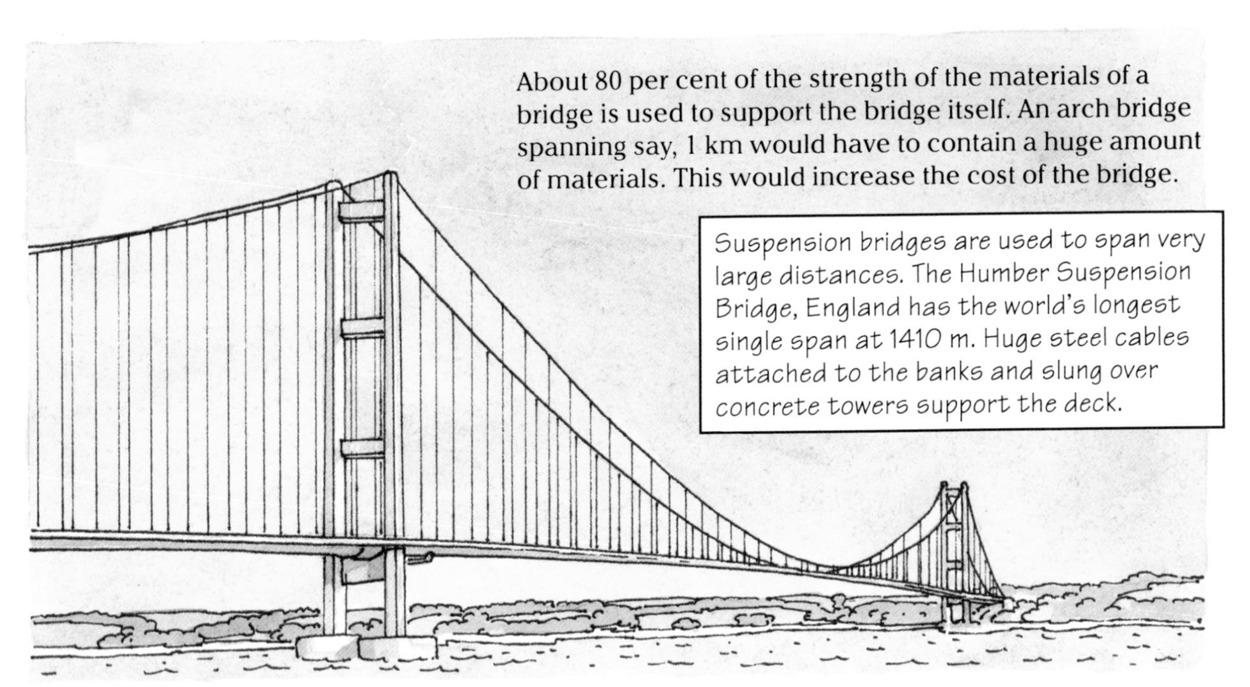

Bridges also have to withstand sideways forces from winds. The centre of the Humber Suspension Bridge is designed to be flexible enough for a sway of 4.5 m.

Which parts of the bridge are under compression?

Which parts are under tension?

Trains must use a less flexible bridge because they need to run on straight rails.

The Forth rail bridge is a cantilever bridge.

Each section of a cantilever bridge is supported by a pillar. The arrangement of girders helps to support the deck and keep it rigid and stable.

The weight applied to any part of the bridge is balanced by the weight of the bridge at another.

SUMMARY

Stone or concrete slab bridges are weak under tension but strong under compression.

Arch bridges can withstand high compression.

Steel is used to make longer arch bridges as it is strong under both compression and tension.

Suspension bridges use the tension strength of steel and the compression strength of concrete.

Cantilever bridges are used where stability is required.

STABILITY

How gravity produces a turning effect on an object

Gravity acts on all parts of an object. The force of gravity acting on an object gives the object its weight.

When carrying a metal bar, you would be able to find a part near the middle of the bar where the weight of the bar on either side of your hand was the same. This point is called the **centre of mass** or **centre of gravity.**

What would happen if you carried the bar at one end?

If you were to hold the bar near to one end, would this make it easier to carry?

If you carry the bar at one end, your hand will act as a pivot and the bar will turn downwards.

Investigation

All objects have a centre of mass. Your centre of mass is near your stomach. When you stand upright, each side of your body is in balance and the effect of your weight is straight downwards between your feet.

Stand upright and keep your feet together. Ask somebody to gently push you over and describe what happens. At what point do you topple over?

Some objects topple over easily. Some do not. The word used to describe the ease or difficulty with which an object topples over is **stability.**

Which of these objects do you think needs the least push to topple it over? Which is the most stable?

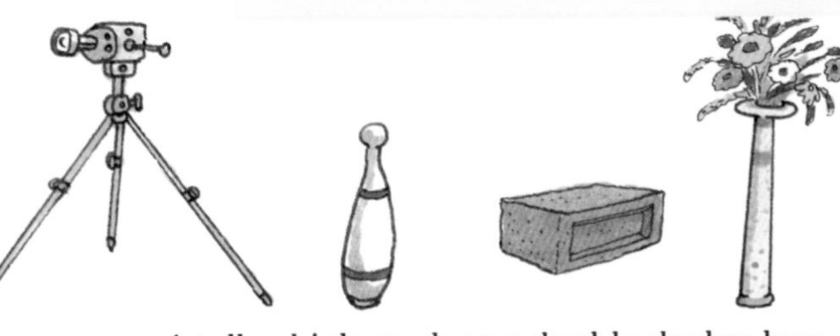

It is important that household appliances such as fridges are stable.

Vehicles need to be stable too.
As a vehicle goes round a corner it has a tendency to topple over.

A tall vehicle such as a double decker bus needs to be designed for as much stability as possible. The weight of the engine is positioned as low down as possible.

Why might the centre of mass of these two buses be at different positions?

Which bus is the most stable? Explain your answer.

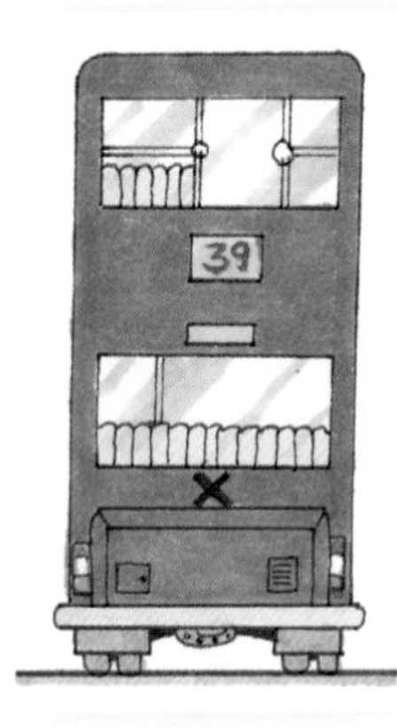

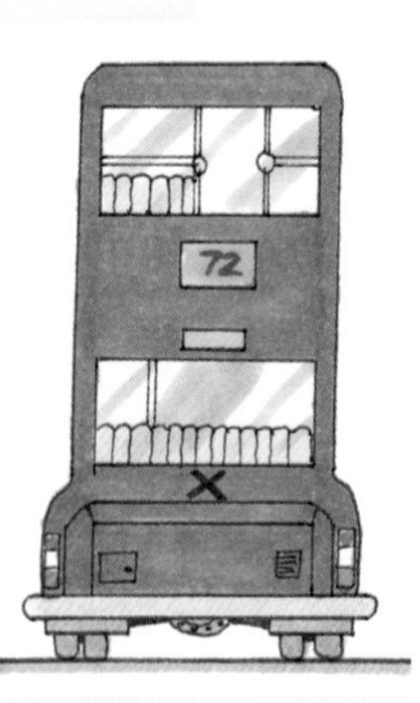

Once the centre of mass passes over the pivot, an object will topple. The lower the centre of mass of an object, the less its tendency to topple over. An object with a low centre of mass is more stable than one with a high centre of mass.

The width of the base of an object also determines its stability. A wide base makes an object more stable.

Which of the buses above is more stable? Explain your answer.

SUMMARY

The point at which the weight of an object seems to act is called its centre of mass or centre of gravity.

When the centre of mass of an object passes over the pivot, the object topples over.

The stability of an object can be increased by lowering the centre of mass.

The stability of an object can be increased by moving the pivot away from the centre of mass, for example, by increasing the width of an object's base.

FORCES AND PRESSURE

The effect of a force spread over an area

When you stand on the ground you are applying a force to the ground. The force is your weight pressing downwards on solid ground. Normally, you can't see the effect of this but in snow you can. You leave footprints.

Why are the bird's tracks not as deep as the footprints?

In deep, soft snow you might sink up to your knees. If you can spread your weight over a larger area, it may stop you sinking. This is why people wear snowshoes. The snowshoes spread their weight over a large area. The pressure on the snow is less with snowshoes than without. Pressure is the force divided by the area on which it is acting.

Two people each have a weight of 500 N. The first is wearing shoes with a total area of 0.1 m^2 and the second is wearing snowshoes with a total area of 0.75 m^2.

What is the force applied by each person on the snow?

What is the pressure exerted by each person on the snow?

Pressure = Force ÷ Area

Blaise Pascal

The standard unit of pressure is the newton per square metre. This unit is called a **pascal (Pa)**. Pascals are named after the French scientist Blaise Pascal (1623–92) who discovered several important principles of pressure.

If an elephant weighing 5000 N had feet with a total area of 1 m^2, what pressure would it be exerting on the ice?

Snowshoes spread weight over a large area and so reduce the pressure on the snow. This effect also works in reverse. A man on stilts standing on snow would sink deeper than a man wearing normal shoes.

Explain why a man on stilts sinks into the snow. Use the words pressure, force and area.

This effect can be useful. The head of a drawing pin has a much larger area than its point. A force on the head of the pin is transferred to the point and the point goes into a pinboard quite easily. Imagine how difficult it would be to push in the pin if its head didn't have a large area.

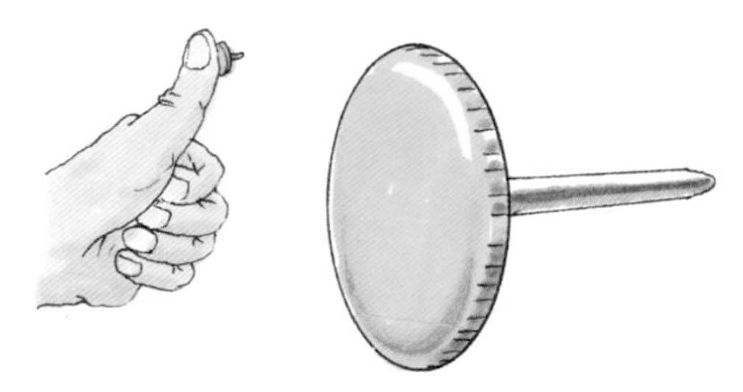

If the force on the head is 10 N, what is the force the point exerts on the pinboard?

If the head has an area of 1 cm^2 and the point has an area of 1 mm^2, what is the pressure on the head and what is the pressure of the point on the wall?

Ice skaters use skates with a narrow edge. When the skates exert a high pressure on the ice, the ice melts and produces a film of water under the skate which makes the ice very slippery.

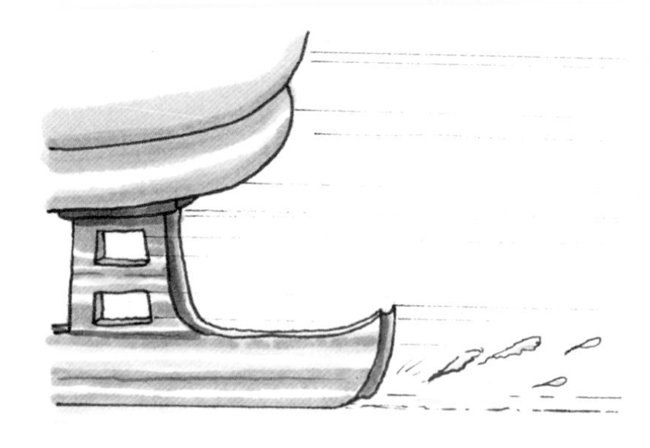

What do you think happens to the film of water when the skate has passed over?

Which of the people in the large picture is exerting the most pressure on the ice, A or B?

SUMMARY

Pressure = Force ÷ Area

The pressure decreases as the area over which a force is applied increases.

The standard unit for pressure is pascals or newtons per square metre.

AIR PRESSURE

How the Earth's atmosphere exerts pressure

Pascal found that the pressure exerted by a liquid or gas acts in all directions in the liquid or gas, and not just downwards. This is shown to the right. This also shows that pressure increases with depth.

Is most pressure being applied at A, B or C?

Why does the water squirt out horizontally from the spouts?

The Earth's atmosphere is about 80 km deep and exerts a huge pressure on our bodies. At sea level this pressure is about 101,325 Pa. In outer space there is no air, and therefore no air pressure. A volume containing nothing is called a **vacuum**.

Calculate the air pressure in newtons per square centimetre.

Why doesn't an umbrella keep air pressure off your head?

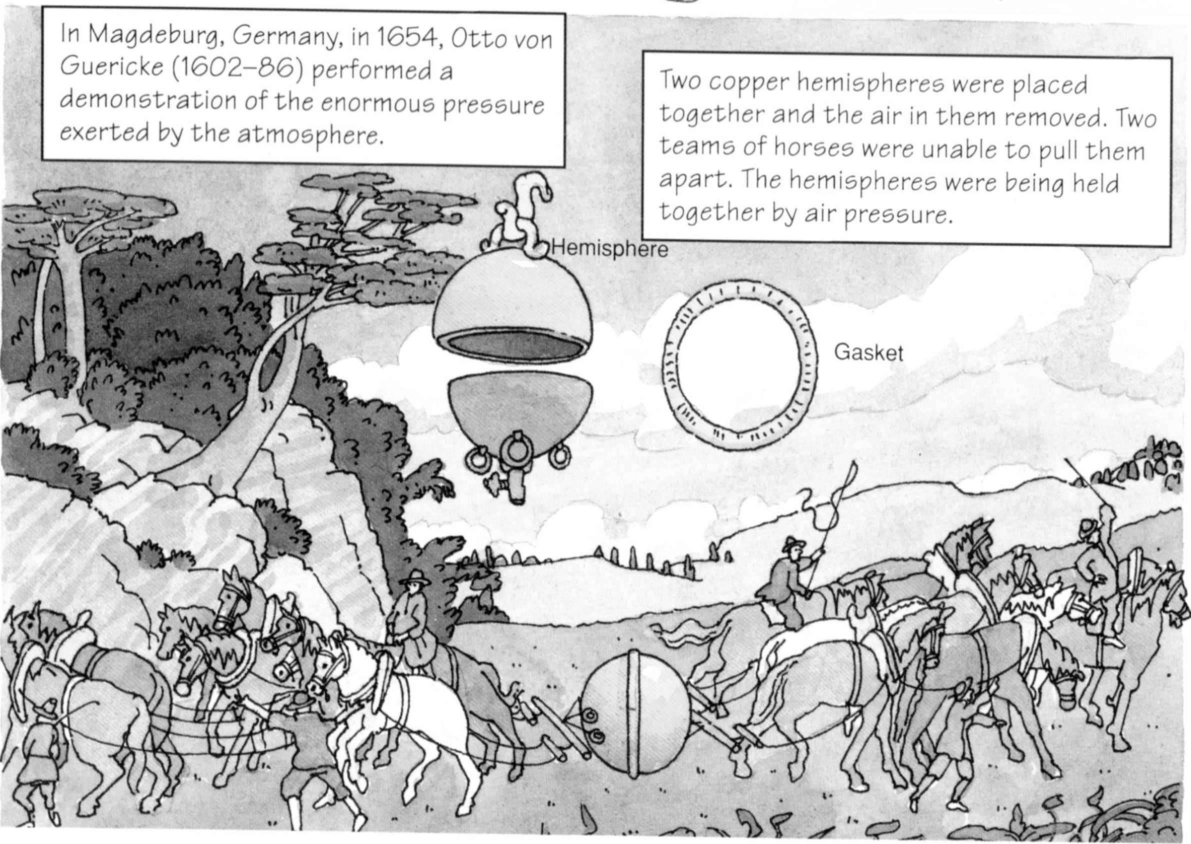

Air pressure forces air in all directions. It will try to force air into any place where there is no air. Another way to say this is that air will try to fill up a vacuum. This effect is useful in many different ways. Even drinking through a straw makes use of air pressure and a vacuum.

When a straw stands in a liquid, the air inside the straw is at the same pressure as the air outside it.

Sucking removes the air from the straw. Air pressure on the liquid's surface can now push liquid into the straw.

Write down other examples where air pressure and a vacuum or partial vacuum are used.

How does a vacuum cleaner pick up dust?

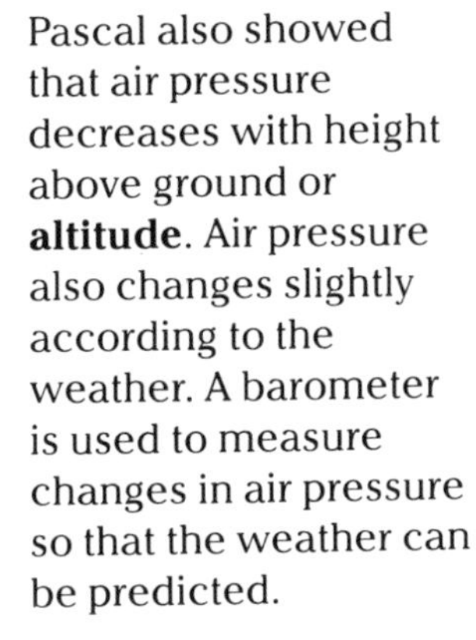

An early English barometer of around 1800

Pascal also showed that air pressure decreases with height above ground or **altitude**. Air pressure also changes slightly according to the weather. A barometer is used to measure changes in air pressure so that the weather can be predicted.

In this simple barometer (right), air pressure on the mercury forces some of it up the tube. The mass of mercury forced into the tube is in direct proportion to the air pressure.

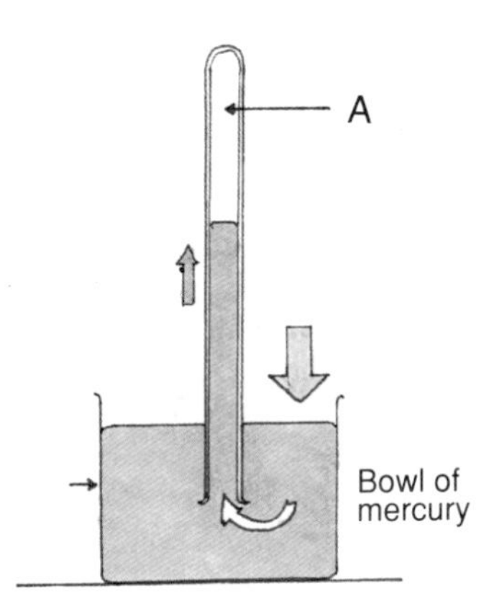

What must be true about the inside of the tube at point A?

If you took a barometer high up in a balloon, would it show a higher or lower reading? Explain your answer.

SUMMARY

Pressure in a liquid or gas acts in all directions.

The atmosphere exerts a huge air pressure.

A volume containing nothing is called a vacuum.

Air pressure tries to force air into a vacuum.

Air pressure can be measured using a barometer.

JOINING FORCES

Combining forces, and equilibrium

When two people are pushing a car, they are each applying a force to the car. Because they are pushing in the same direction, the forces can be added together to find the **resultant force.**
For example, two people each applying a force of 500 N would have the same effect as one person applying a force of 1000 N.

What would happen to the car if the people were pushing in opposite directions?

When forces act in opposite directions, the resultant force is found by subtracting the smaller force from the larger. For example, if a box is being pushed across the floor with a force of 200 N and there is a force due to friction of 150 N acting in the opposite direction, the resultant force will be a force of 50 N.

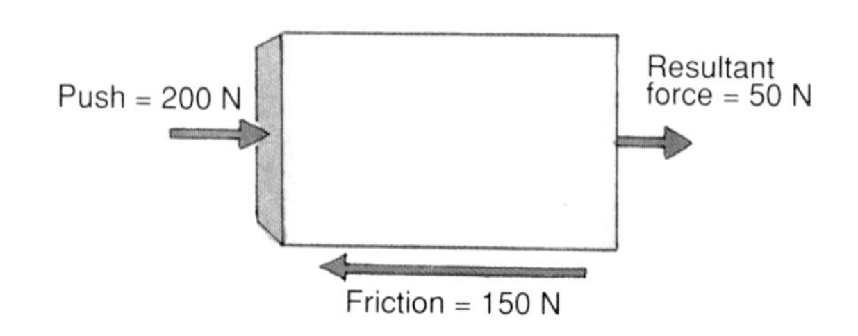

In which direction is the resultant force acting?

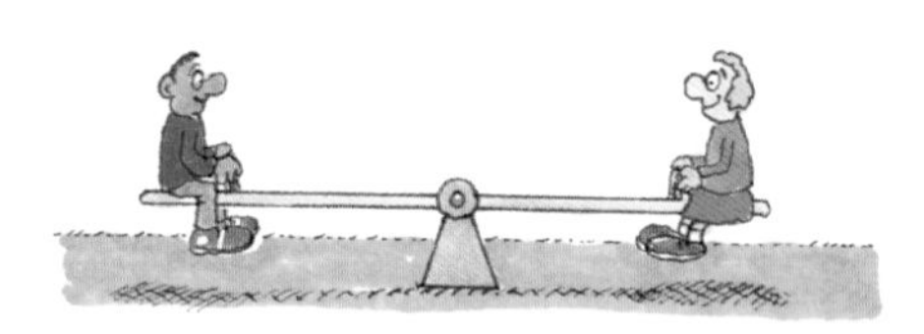

This see-saw to the left isn't moving. What can you say about the moments of the forces due to the weight of the two children?

If two forces act on an object so that they balance each other out, the object is said to be in **equilibrium**. That is, the object doesn't move because the resultant force is 0 N.

When two children sit on a see-saw, there is a moment of force due to the weight of each child. The see-saw will move in the direction of the largest moment.

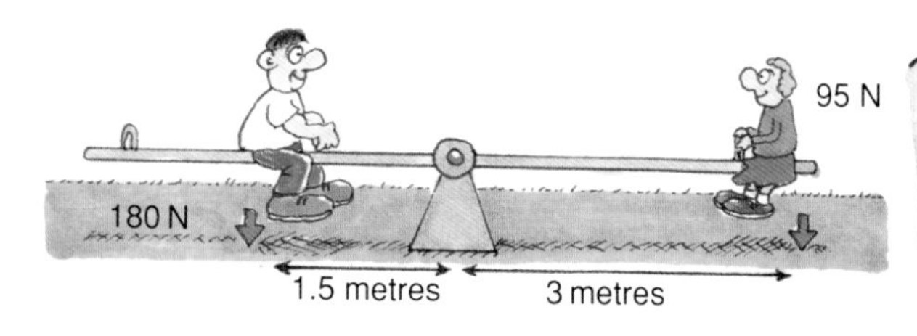

Which way will the see-saw move? Explain your answer.

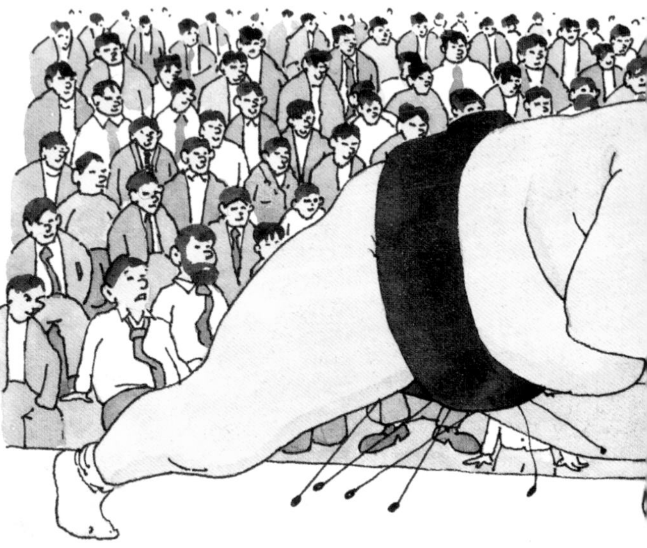

Each of these sumo wrestlers applies huge forces against the other. Sometimes their forces cancel each other out – they are in equilibrium.

These removers have left a heavy wardrobe on the ramp of their van while they have a cup of tea.

What force is trying to make the wardrobe slide down the ramp?

What force is holding the wardrobe in position?

If the slope were steeper, might it still stay in position?

Is the wardrobe in equilibrium?

In this case, there are three forces acting on the wardrobe. There is the weight of the wardrobe, the friction between the ramp and the wardrobe, and the support of the ramp. The wardrobe does not move because they all balance each other out.

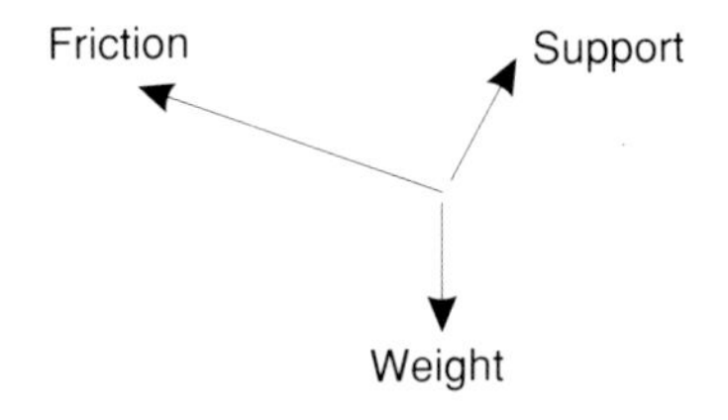

A diagram of forces can be drawn to help visualize what might happen to an object with many forces acting on it.

A hummingbird can hover in one position whilst it sips nectar from a flower. It creates an upwards force by flapping its wings up to 80 times a second. This force balances the downwards force due to gravity and keeps the bird in equilibrium.

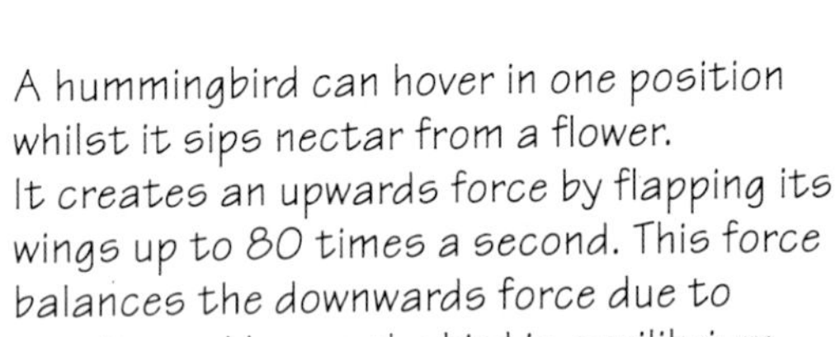

SUMMARY

Two or more forces can be combined to give a resultant force.

If the forces acting on an object balance each other, the object is said to be in equilibrium.

The direction of the forces acting on an object can be drawn to help visualize the motion or equilibrium which might result.

FORCE, MASS AND DENSITY

What mass consists of and how forces affect it

Mass is the quantity of matter in an object,and is measured in **kilograms (kg)**.

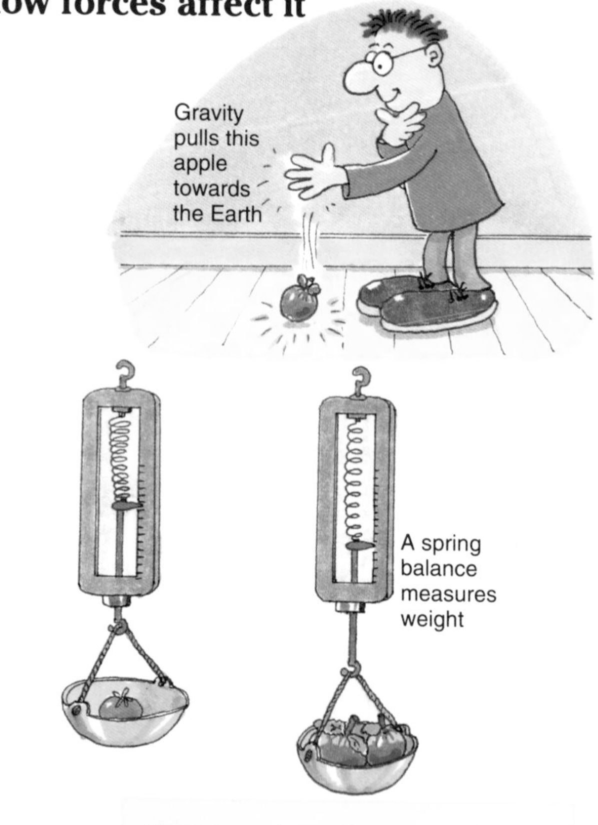

Objects have weight because gravity pulls the objects towards the Earth. Weight is measured in newtons.

The weight of an object can be measured by a spring balance marked with weight values in newtons.

Gravity on the Moon is only one-sixth that of the Earth's. This means that on the Moon, objects will weigh one-sixth of their weight on the Earth.

Mass is not a force. An object's mass does not change. It is the same wherever you go in the universe.

An object's mass cannot be measured by a spring balance as this would give different results depending on the force due to gravity. Instead, mass is measured on a beam balance which is a device like a see-saw. Using a beam balance, an object's mass is measured by comparing it to a standard mass. This will give the same result no matter what the force is due to gravity.

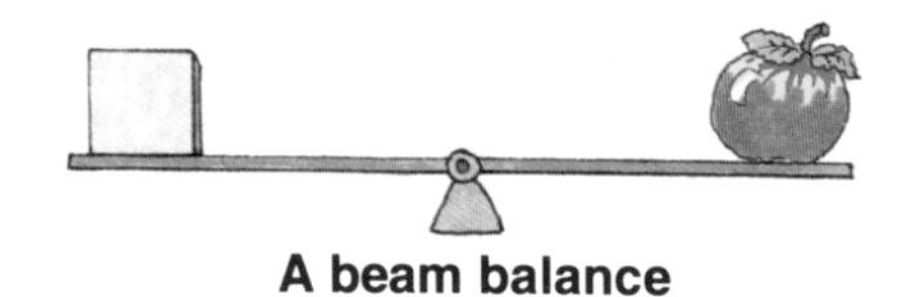

A beam balance

If the mass of the apple were measured on the Moon using the beam balance, it would be the same as on the Earth.

In outer space, objects are weightless. This astronaut is floating in space and is not falling in any direction.

What is the astronaut's weight in newtons? What force is not acting on the astronaut? What would happen to the apple if she let it go?

The apple is weightless. If the astronaut throws the apple, do you think it will be damaged when it hits the spaceship? Explain your answer.

The **volume** of an object is the amount of space which it occupies. The units of volume are cubic centimetres (cc or cm^3).

The **density** of an object is a measure of how much matter is contained in a given volume. The units for density are grammes per cm^3.

Density = Mass ÷ Volume

If the mass of the apple is 0.1 kg and its volume is 0.25 litres, what is its density? What is the density of the same volume of airless space?

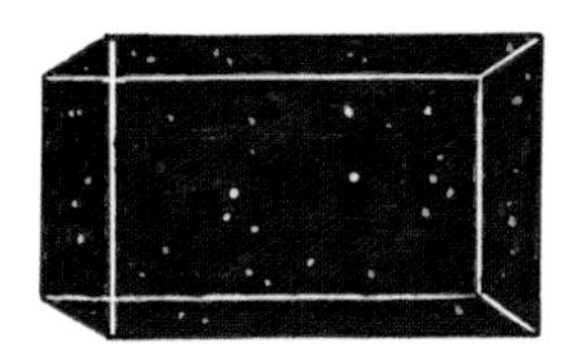

SUMMARY

The mass of an object is measured in kilograms.

Forces acting on a mass can be measured in newtons by using a spring balance.

Gravity is a force which gives objects weight.

An object's weight changes if it is taken to a place where gravity is different.

An object's mass remains the same wherever it is.

Density = mass ÷ volume

BUOYANCY

How different things have different abilities to float

Here are three identical rubber balls floating in three different liquids. The density of each ball is the same, but the three liquids have different densities. The downwards force of the ball is the same in each case.

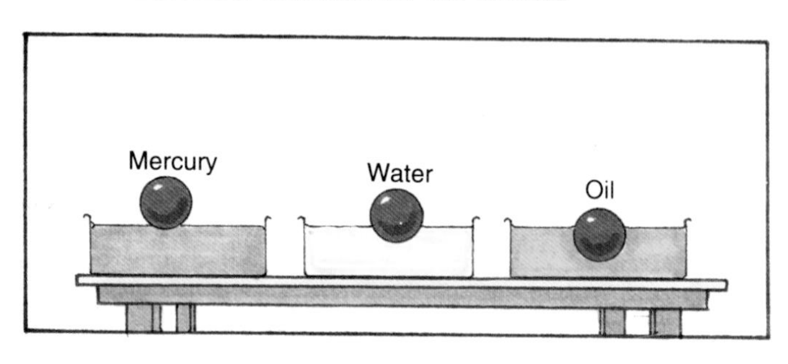

The more dense a liquid is, the more upward force it exerts. The more dense an object floating in the liquid is, the more downward force it exerts. When the downward force of an object is greater than the upward force of a liquid, the object sinks. **Buoyancy** is the measure of an object's ability to float.

What force is supporting the balls?

Do you think the upward force of each liquid is different or the same?

Which liquid has the greatest upward force?

Some objects might float or sink depending on their shape.

An aluminium tray will float on water but if it is screwed up tightly into a ball it will sink.

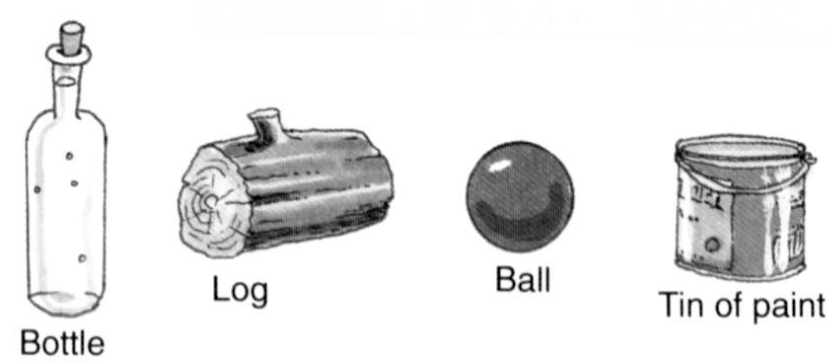

The objects above all have equal volume. Which of them do you think are more dense than water? Which will sink?

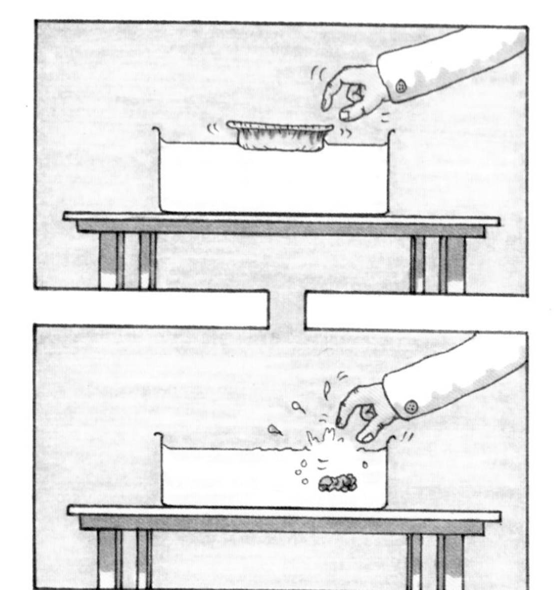

Aluminium is more dense than water. Why do you think the aluminium tray floats?
How does the air in the tray affect its overall density?

The shape of an object of any material, however heavy, can be modified to allow it to float. Fully laden, the world's largest cargo ship, *Berge Stahl*, has a mass of 330,850 tonnes (1 tonne = 1000 kg). If it were crushed into a solid block, it would sink.

A ship floats because it contains air. The overall density of the materials from which the ship is made together with the air which the ship contains is less than the density of water.

SUMMARY

A floating object exerts a downwards pressure on a liquid.

This is balanced by an upward pressure from the liquid.

Filling an object (which would normally sink) with air reduces its density and allows it to float.

DESIGNING BOATS

How forces and friction affect the design of vehicles

A weightless spaceship travelling through a vacuum encounters no friction. Once it has been set in motion it will never stop unless it hits something, such as a planet.

Why don't all the projecting instruments on this space probe slow it down?

Here is a small motor boat. The propeller is moving the boat forward through the water at a steady speed. If the sailor switches off the motor, the force exerted by the propeller becomes zero. The boat would slow down, then stop.

What force is resisting the boat's motion through the water?

Let's suppose instead of switching off, the sailor applies more power to the motor. More force will then be exerted by the propeller.

Will the boat slow down, accelerate or swerve to one side?

An object, such as a boat, will go faster if the force pushing it is increased. However an accelerating boat is trying to push more and more water out of its way every second. At some point, the motor will no longer be able to push any extra water out of the way. Then the boat stops accelerating and maintains a steady speed.

What stops a boat accelerating?

Some boats are specially designed to go fast. Powerboats are used for racing.

In what way is a powerboat shaped differently to the motor boat?

How do you think the shape helps to reduce friction?

Is a powerboat's motor likely to be more or less powerful than the motor boat's?

Here is a rowing boat. The oars are acting as levers and are pivoted on the side of the boat. The rower is rowing as hard as he can to overcome the current but he is not moving. The force the oars are exerting is equal and opposite to the force of the current.

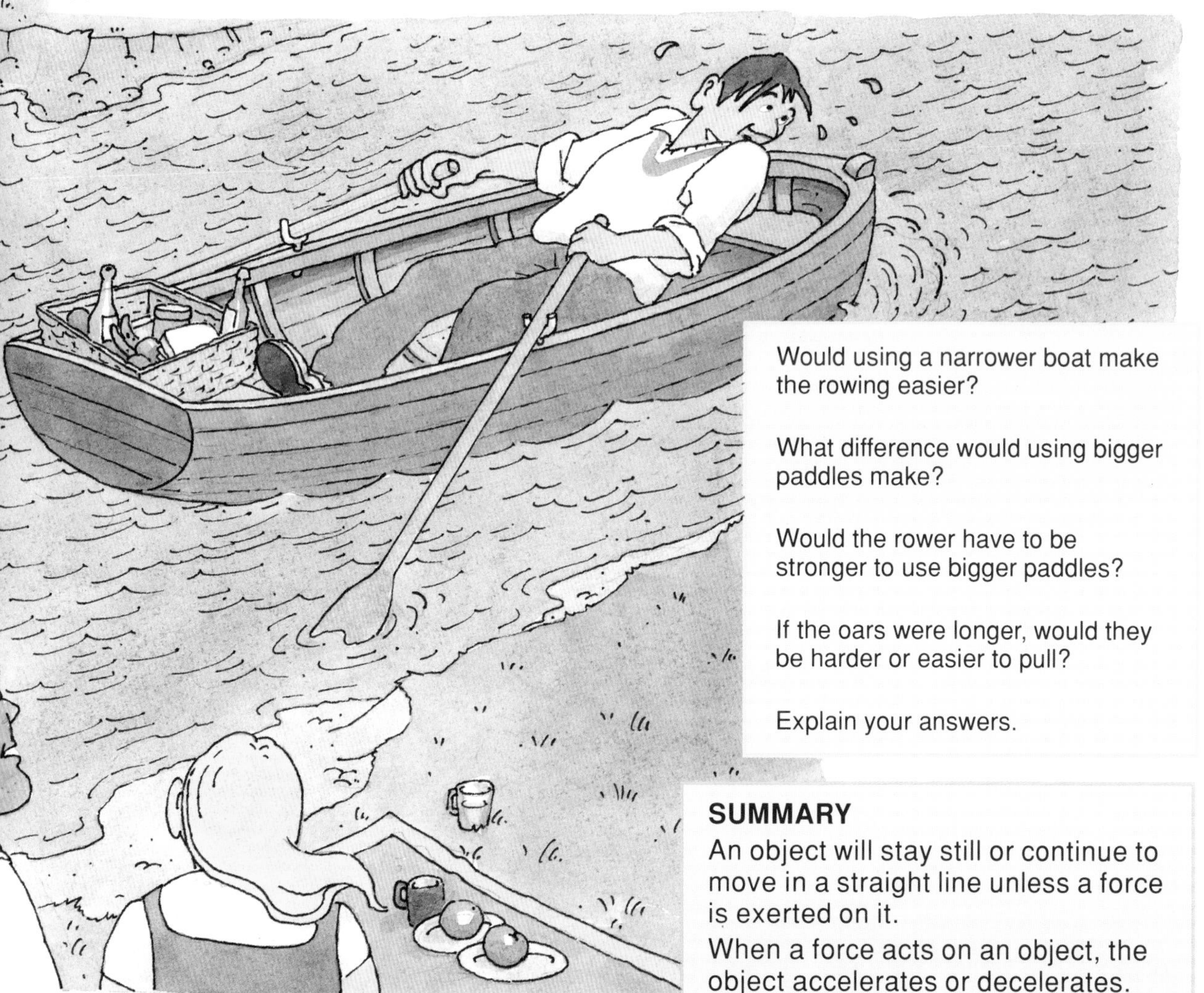

Would using a narrower boat make the rowing easier?

What difference would using bigger paddles make?

Would the rower have to be stronger to use bigger paddles?

If the oars were longer, would they be harder or easier to pull?

Explain your answers.

SUMMARY

An object will stay still or continue to move in a straight line unless a force is exerted on it.

When a force acts on an object, the object accelerates or decelerates.

Key words appear in **bold** the first time they occur in the text.

INDEX

Published by Heinemann Library,
an imprint of Heinemann Publishers (Oxford) Ltd,
Halley Court, Jordan Hill, Oxford, OX2 8EJ

OXFORD LONDON EDINBURGH
MADRID PARIS ATHENS BOLOGNA
MELBOURNE SYDNEY AUCKLAND SINGAPORE
TOKYO IBADAN NAIROBI GABORONE HARARE
PORTSMOUTH NH (USA)

First published 1994
98 97
10 9 8 7 6 5 4 3 2
British Library Cataloguing Publication in Data
is available on request from the British Library.
ISBN 0-431-07602-2 (HB)
ISBN 0-431-07567-0 (PB)
Designed by Lazy Summer Books Ltd.
Illustrated by Lazy Summer Books Ltd.
Printed in Hong Kong by Wing King Tong Co. Ltd.